Uncommon Meetings

By

Ann Latham

Uncommon Meetings

7 Quick Tips for Better Results in Half the Time

Ann Latham

RED OAK HILL
PRESS

Red Oak Hill Press Second Edition, August 2011

UNCOMMON MEETINGS

ISBN: 978-0-9824684-4-9

eISBN: 978-0-9824684-5-6

Printed in the United States of America.

The first edition, released in 2010, was called "The Meeting Clarity Handbook – 7 Quick Tips for Better Results in Half the Time" and was sold as a PDF with ISBN: 978-1-6106800-7-3.

Dedicated to all the people who are tired of spending countless wasteful hours in minimally productive meetings and are ready to do something about it.

Contents

Introduction

Many employees spend up to half their time in meetings. If this is the average, that means the equivalent of half of the company's employees do nothing but attend meetings. For some companies, the number is even higher. How many of your employees are effectively employed just to attend meetings?

Now imagine what it would be like if you cut all your meetings in half. Imagine how many "new workers" you would gain! Imagine recovering big chunks of your day and maybe even leaving work at a reasonable hour! Imagine how much money you could save!

I've never met a meeting that couldn't be reduced by 25%. Taking 15 minutes out of the average one-hour meeting is surprisingly easy. And taking 30 minutes out of each hour is a lot easier than you think.

Not only can you shorten meetings, you can also decrease the number of meetings. Meetings chop employee days into little segments; this is not the road to productivity and employee satisfaction. Furthermore, ineffective meetings generate interpersonal conflict and damage morale.

If you would like to get better results in half the time, follow the seven tips below and start taking back those wasted hours today!

#1—Outcomes, Outcomes, Outcomes!

In real estate, the mantra is "location, location, location!" When it comes to meetings, the mantra must be "outcomes, outcomes, outcomes!" If you can clarify your expected outcomes, you have taken the first and biggest step toward better results in half the time.

Most meeting agendas identify activities, not outcomes. Here are typical examples of activities that guarantee time will be wasted:

- Discuss
- Report
- Communicate

In these examples, how will anyone ever know when the meeting is over?

Many agendas don't even use verbs. They just list topics:

- Project Xanadu
- Financials
- Employee satisfaction

These, like the previous examples, are invitations to ramble. The talkative will be unleashed and the introverts will sit in silence, waiting for the clue that lets them make a positive contribution.

To establish clear outcomes, answer these questions:

- What will be different when the meeting is over?

- What will have been decided, planned, created, or resolved?

- How will you know when you are finished?

- What step will have been completed so another step can proceed?

If you spend just a few minutes trying to transform a typical agenda item into an outcome, you will gain greater insight into why most agendas open the flood gates that wash away the hours. For example, take "Discuss Plan." Why might you discuss a plan? What might be the point? Here are a few outcome-based alternatives:

- Present the plan and identify and assign actions that must be taken this week

- Present the plan, identify risks, and determine ways to mitigate the most serious risks

- Present the plan and identify significant gaps so the plan can be completed

- Present the plan and brainstorm implementation methods

Each of these examples provides a clear focus and each is easily assessed for completeness. Furthermore, each provokes a totally different discussion. If your objective is simply to "discuss plan," there is no way to know when you are finished.

Outcomes, outcomes, outcomes! Don't call a meeting until you are clear about what will be different when the meeting is over. Challenge yourself to define specific outcomes for every standing meeting you regularly attend.

Avoid Treadmill Verbs (activities which are potentially endless)	Identify Outcomes (so you know when you are done)
• Discuss • Report • Review • Explain • Present • Communicate	• Decisions • Agreement • Plans • Solutions • Assignments • Definitions • A list of ideas, answers, questions, candidates, etc. • All questions answered

#2—Worthy Outcomes

While establishing clear outcomes is the first and most important step to better results in half the time, it is not sufficient. You may be clear about what you want to achieve but that doesn't mean your proposed outcome is worthy of investment, especially the level of investment required when convening a meeting. Thus, your proposed outcome must pass three tests of worthiness. Before scheduling a meeting, check the following:

Right Focus:
- Will achieving your desired outcomes support an important organizational objective?

Right Level of Investment:
- What level of investment makes sense?
- How many hours and people is it worth?
- Do you really need to involve more people and devote more time to move forward?
- What constitutes 'good enough'?

Right Way to Achieve Outcomes:
- Is a meeting the best way to achieve each outcome?
- Do you need group interaction to obtain results?
- Will a meeting reduce total time?
- Will it be hard to achieve the outcomes without being face-to-face?

So if you have a worthy objective and you need the interaction to get the level of results required and/or you believe you will save time overall and/or you think that stronger relationships are important to success, call a meeting! Otherwise, skip it! Here are

some alternatives:
- If you want to dispense information, use written communication or an audio or video recording.
- If the issue is not very important, drop it entirely, do it alone, or scale back on involving others and move on.
- If more effort will not necessarily produce better results, e.g., you are choosing among alternatives with minimal long term difference, do it alone or scale back on involving others.
- If broader input is needed or a second set of eyes would reduce risk, collect input or feedback via a phone call, email, one-on-one exchange, an online forum, etc.
- If interaction is important for achieving results or saving time, consider a conference call, videoconference, or active forum to save the travel or gathering time required for a meeting (IBM holds conference calls within a facility so people have ready access to notes, files, computer, etc.).

At this point, if you are still planning to call a meeting, let's hope it is for all the right reasons.

---

1. Devote effort and time only in proportion to the value of your desired outcome.
2. Call a meeting only if you think it will:
   - Reduce total time spent achieving the outcome
   - Improve results in an important way
   - Build relationships necessary for strong results

#3—A Roadmap

The third critical step to getting better results in half the time is to identify the shortest path from where you are now to your desired outcomes. This roadmap to your destination is simply a series of intermediate outcomes, each of which gets you closer to your destination and each of which passes the test for a meeting outcome.

Thus, if you were able to establish meeting outcomes, you should be able to establish intermediate outcomes. What do you need to decide, plan, create, or uncover in order to achieve each desired outcome? Each step completed paves the way for another step. Identifying these steps ensures progress before, during, and after each meeting.

The first and most obvious advantage of a clear roadmap is that it makes it easy to keep everyone focused throughout the meeting.

The second benefit of a clear roadmap is that every meeting becomes a greater success. If you don't reach your desired outcome for some reason, you should have at least reached several intermediate outcomes and be clear about next steps. This is not the case when you "discuss" or "communicate."

For example, suppose your roadmap – your series of intermediate outcomes is:

- Communicate the decision
- Answer all questions

- Determine next steps

- Assign action items

Now suppose you never finished the second item because there were many more good and important questions than you anticipated. Assuming another meeting makes sense so that everyone can continue to hear all questions and answers, it is easy enough to resume right where you left off at another meeting.

The third advantage of a roadmap consisting of intermediate outcomes is that it is easy to tell when each is achieved so you can keep making progress throughout the meeting. "Have I answered all questions?" "Do we agree that these are the four steps that must be taken now?" "Has each been assigned with a deadline?" Since each has an endpoint, you can check them off decisively as you pursue the final destination.

The fourth advantage of a clear roadmap helps you overcome one of the biggest stumbling blocks for meetings and that is a lack of agreement over the starting point.

For example, suppose you are leading the meeting with the roadmap enumerated above. You expect to quickly communicate a decision and then answer questions. If you aren't clear and firm about the fact that the decision has already been made – about your starting point, the group can go in any number of directions, including re-making the decision, questioning the need for a decision, and more. If you are clear about the starting point, you should be able to react effectively to the only three scenarios that can follow:

- You communicate the decision and proceed to #2 and answer questions

- You communicate the decision, people protest, you reaffirm the decision, and move forward with answers to questions

- You communicate the decision, people protest, you have second thoughts about the decision, and take an intentional detour to re-consider the decision.

Even the latter is far preferable to letting the conversation wander around in a decision that has already been made.

In the first of our seven tips, we stressed the importance of "outcomes, outcomes, outcomes." A roadmap consisting of intermediate outcomes is just as critical for all the same reasons. Challenge yourself to create a roadmap that will get you to your destination in half the usual time allotted, 15 minutes, not 30; 30 minutes, not 60.

> The Roadmap: A list of necessary, intermediate outcomes that ensure progress toward the ultimate desired outcomes.

#4—The Right People

Ensure the right people are at your meeting. Too often the same old crew is invited or a "just in case" mentality leads to a long list of attendees. With your roadmap in hand, there is no excuse for thoughtlessly wasting other people's time.

To identify the right people, turn to your roadmap. Examine each step and consider the following:

- From whom can you obtain the needed expertise, insights, agreement, and commitment?
- Who has the authority to make decisions and commitments related to your outcomes?
- If you need input and commitment from a group, who can reasonably represent that group?
- If you need preparation, what will that look like, who can provide it, and when is it needed?
- What will you do if one or more key people are unavailable or drop out at the last minute? Can you identify alternates? Do you need double coverage? Will you postpone the meeting?
- Have you identified too many players to be effective? If so, modify the roadmap or shorten the list. Remember to balance time and effort with benefit.

For each step in your Roadmap, determine from whom you need: Input, Commitment, and Authorization

#5—Prepared People

The fifth step for getting better results in half the time is to be sure attendees are prepared.

- Why do you want them present?
- What do you expect of each before and during the meeting?
- Whom are they representing, if anyone?
- What expertise are you expecting each to provide?
- What is the best way to inform them of their roles?
- Will you need to follow up?

Never assume that because someone is present he is representing the point of view or taking the role you desire. He could be considering the issue at hand from a different perspective than you wish (e.g., from the customer's point of view, not your company's ability to deliver). Also, never assume that a lack of protest means agreement. The silent one may be thinking about the project left behind on his desk and its pending deadline or may be too irate to speak up. Just as your best hope for quick assistance in a medical emergency is to point to an individual and say, "You! Call 911!" your best hope for strong participation in a meeting is to be equally explicit as to why each individual has been invited.

Attendees
• Show up
• Listen, at least mostly
• Participate, if the topic is of interest

Prepared Participants
• Know what to do beforehand and do it
• Know why they are there, whom they are representing, and what they are expected to contribute
• Are as committed to achieving the outcomes quickly as the leader

#6—A Strong Leader

Now that you know exactly what you are trying to achieve, have a roadmap for getting there, and have lined up the people you need to be successful, the sixth step to getting better results in half the time lands on your shoulders as the leader (or on whomever will be leading the meeting). As the leader, you must be able to:

- Maintain the group's focus

- Follow your roadmap

- Adjust for unexpected circumstances

- Finish on time

Given the seriousness and complexity of the situation, your capabilities, and the characteristics of the group, think seriously about what you will need to succeed.

You may need:

- Rough timeframes for each step so you can monitor progress

- Firm commitments from those taking over portions of the meeting to ensure they won't exceed allotted times

- Permission from the group to interrupt so you feel comfortable regardless of rank to interrupt when necessary and do your best to move the meeting along

- Someone else to watch the clock, to cut off needless debate, or to remind you to get back on topic
- A plan for controlling someone who has a tendency to dominate or get nasty
- Ground rules, like no cell phones, to prevent delays, distractions, and problems
- A sense of humor
- A min/max plan so you don't feel so pressured when things don't go according to plan
- A facilitator so you can concentrate on content and don't have to worry about the clock and the process
- A professional facilitator to get the most out of the attendees, stay on schedule, navigate complex topics, and handle difficult people and group dynamics, etc.

Strong leaders anticipate and prepare to ensure they can achieve:

- Focus
- Progress
- Adjustments
- On-time completion

#7—A Framework of Meetings

Meetings should not be popping up around the organization like dandelions in a field. So while the first six steps will help you get better results in half the time, your biggest opportunity may lie in your management system. Most meetings should be part of a predictable process within which goals are established, plans are laid, resources are allocated, progress is tracked, and adjustments are made.

Without a decent framework, people scramble to do their jobs and rush around to too many meetings. Poorly planned meetings crop up to plug the gaps in ill-defined priorities, ad hoc processes, inadequate plans, and insufficient resources. Every business needs a simple framework of meetings, each with a well-defined purpose, to manage the business as a whole and each of its projects and initiatives.

But be careful. Management systems can lead to a lot of standing meetings. You never want to meet just because it is Tuesday morning. If attendees can't explain the expected outcomes of a standing meeting and don't believe the benefits outweigh the costs, that standing meeting should be cancelled until further notice.

Meetings pop up like dandelions when:	Meetings as part of a predictable management process
• Problems occur • Employees get stuck • Previous meetings are unsuccessful • Arguments erupt	• Establish goals • Lay Plans • Allocates Resources • Track Progress • Make Adjustments to Plans

Are You Ready for Your Next Meeting?

1. Have you identified your desired outcomes? Are you clear about what will be different when the meeting ends?

2. Have you thought about how much time and effort should be devoted to achieving these outcomes? Will a meeting save total time, provide necessary improvements in results, and/or build relationships needed to achieve reasonable results?

3. Do you have a roadmap? Have you identified the intermediate outcomes that will get you to your desired outcomes?

4. Have you identified the people from whom you need input, authorization, and commitment?

5. Do the identified people know what is expected of them before and during the meeting so that you can achieve your desired outcomes?

6. Do you know what you need to do to be successful as the meeting leader?

7. Is this meeting part of a predictable management process? If not, why not?

About the Author

Ann Latham creates clarity.

As a consultant, Ann creates the clarity that helps corporate giants like Hitachi and Boeing achieve superior results faster and with greater confidence. She also helps smaller businesses and non-profits see their organizations, people, opportunities, and next steps in clear and new ways. Ann's clarity has contributed to the success of organizations with a wide range of specialties.

As a master facilitator, Ann creates the clarity that ensures teams find common ground, develop a shared vision, and make dramatic progress toward achieving their objectives.

As a coach, Ann helps individuals maximize their impact and opportunities.

As a writer, Ann creates clarity for thousands worldwide who have discovered the value in her *Clear Thoughts*™ newsletter, books, articles, and comments in publications such as *The New York Times*, *Forbes*, *BusinessWeek*, and *Inc*.

As a speaker, Ann creates clarity for audiences who want clear, pragmatic, immediately applicable ideas. Her value-packed and entertaining presentations, whether to small CEO roundtables, students of organizational behavior, or large business gatherings, inevitably garner enthusiastic reviews along with statements of "she really is uncommonly clear."

Not surprisingly, Ann is also the president of Uncommon Clarity, Inc., a consulting firm that creates the clarity that dramatically speeds and improves results.

For more information or to sign up for her complimentary newsletter, visit www.UncommonClarity.com

Companion Audio Seminar

by Ann Latham

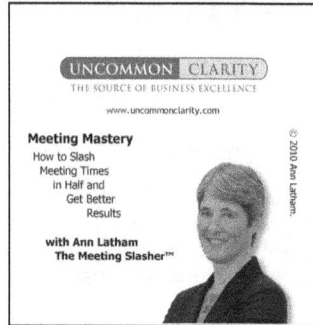

UNCOMMON CLARITY
THE SOURCE OF BUSINESS EXCELLENCE
www.uncommonclarity.com

Meeting Mastery
How to Slash
Meeting Times
in Half and
Get Better
Results

© 2010 Ann Latham.

with Ann Latham
The Meeting Slasher™

Meeting Mastery

How to Slash Meeting Times in Half and Get Better Results

Want to double productivity? Spending too much of your week in meetings? Tired of meetings that just lead to more meetings? Want to take back those meeting hours so you can do something else with your day or leave work at a more reasonable hour?

Then this audio seminar by master facilitator and performance improvement expert Ann Latham, a.k.a., The Meeting Slasher™, is for you!

In this 45-minute audio seminar, you will learn:

- The six secrets to slashing meeting times in half and getting better results
- The three critical criteria for holding a meeting
- How to recognize meetings that should be eliminated
- Techniques that will make you a better meeting leader today
- How to recognize trouble on an agenda and intervene to minimize wasted time
- How you, as a participant, can speed and improve results
- When ground rules are needed and which are most helpful

Available in CD or MP3 formats.

Order now at www.uncommonclarity.com or by calling 800-527-0087.

Also by Ann Latham

Clear Thoughts
- Pragmatic Gems of Better
Business Thinking

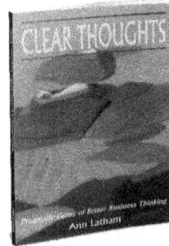

Clear Thoughts - Pragmatic Gems of Better Business Thinking, contains thirty-two concise articles that will provoke, motivate and provide immediately applicable advice for getting better results.

Learn how you can:
- Accelerate progress
- Boost productivity, and
- Capitalize on talent

Readers will come back to these thoughts and tips again and again. Each is a quick read. Each provides great value.

A few sample titles:
- Keep Your Mission to Yourself!
- No Geeks? No Geniuses? No Problem!
- The Stop-Doing List
- Lazy? Incompetent? Clueless?
- Multi-tasking Can Kill Productivity, Quality, and People

All books come with a complimentary Uncommon Clarity bookmark packed with helpful tips.

Order now at www.uncommonclarity.com or by calling 800-527-0087.

What Others Say
about Ann Latham

"On a collaborative project with Boeing Phantom Works, Ann did a tremendous job in identifying the cost drivers, producibility issues, and productivity barriers of a supplier organization, all of which were impeding the success of our project. With Ann helping to provide the focus and oversight, the supplier was able to meet their commitments for quality, cost, and schedule."

Ed Gerding, Chief Engineer C-17 St. Louis,
The Boeing Company

"Ann's ability to simplify complex issues such that everyone understood their respective roles was a key part of her success. She truly helped us achieve profitable and predictable growth while improving the quality of our methods and processes."

S. W. Emery, Jr., Chairman and CEO,
MTS Systems Corporation

"Ann Latham transformed our thinking about how our organization works. This discovery led us to a strategic model that solves our pain and opens new opportunities. She truly lives up to her brand of 'uncommon clarity.'"

Suzanne Beck, Executive Director,
Greater Northampton Chamber of Commerce

"Thank you, Ann, for two great days. You are clearly a gifted facilitator and helped us achieve some important outcomes, both in terms of a strategy for the future and our ability to work more collaboratively together. The ROI was there."

Bob Fazzi, President & CEO, Fazzi Associates

"Ann recognizes that "best practice" may not be "best approach" for her clients, and when it is not, her working knowledge of alternative approaches will result in a solution that will be better than "best" because it works for you, in your plant, with your people.

"Ann can help you identify the crux of a problem and solutions that will work for you. While others may be good, my 35 years of experience tells me that no one is better."

Perry Walraven, President and CEO,
Performance Controls, Inc.,
a subsidiary of Hitachi Medical Corporation

"Ann does a great job of keeping people focused, cutting to the critical issues, and avoiding 'rabbit holes.' I would recommend her to anyone who wants to make better plans and decisions in less time and with better confidence in the outcomes."

W. Lowell Putnam, Chairman/CSO, VCI

"Ann is simply outstanding at moving a group to a strong conclusion. In our case, I couldn't have imagined a better outcome. What makes her particularly unusual is that there isn't a lot of noise, she doesn't distract, and no one wastes time. She lets discussions run but doesn't let them run amok. She is deliberate and straight forward with a soft touch that keeps people on task, the process moving forward, and ideas flowing. By always maintaining a clear purpose, next steps, and expectations, she made me a better contributor and able to get on task quickly despite the limited time I had for the project. After working with Ann, I wouldn't hesitate to recommend her to anyone in need of a strategy, plan, arbitration, facilitation, etc."

Chuck McCullagh, CFO, The Williston Northampton School

"Ann is an excellent facilitator of ideas and issues. She has the capacity to get people to think about change, even when they are more than satisfied with the status quo. Her work with us helped change the direction of three units very set in their ways and has opened up a myriad of possibilities for growth in the future."

Joan Schuman, Executive Director,
Hampshire Educational Collaborative

"'Wow' sums it up nicely. Ann stepped into a delicate, sensitive situation involving a diverse, disjointed group of people with a challenging objective and, in remarkably little time, moved us to a solid, shared conclusion. The way she works is impressive: she has a great handle on people, makes everyone want to work together, ensures every meeting is focused and valuable, and simplifies issues so all understand the challenges and options and can reach shared conclusions. On top of that, I really enjoy working with her."

John Heaps, President, Florence Savings Bank

"Having worked with Ann on multiple projects, I know to expect a lot. Nonetheless, she continues to exceed expectations. Ann gets people out of their comfort zones, thinking, and seeing other points of view. She manages somehow to turn personal agendas aside and create powerful teams. She is always well prepared and willing to take charge to ensure we accomplish what needs to be accomplished in a timely fashion. In addition, she is personable and articulate. I highly recommend her services."

William F. Dimmitt, Account Executive, The AXiA
Group